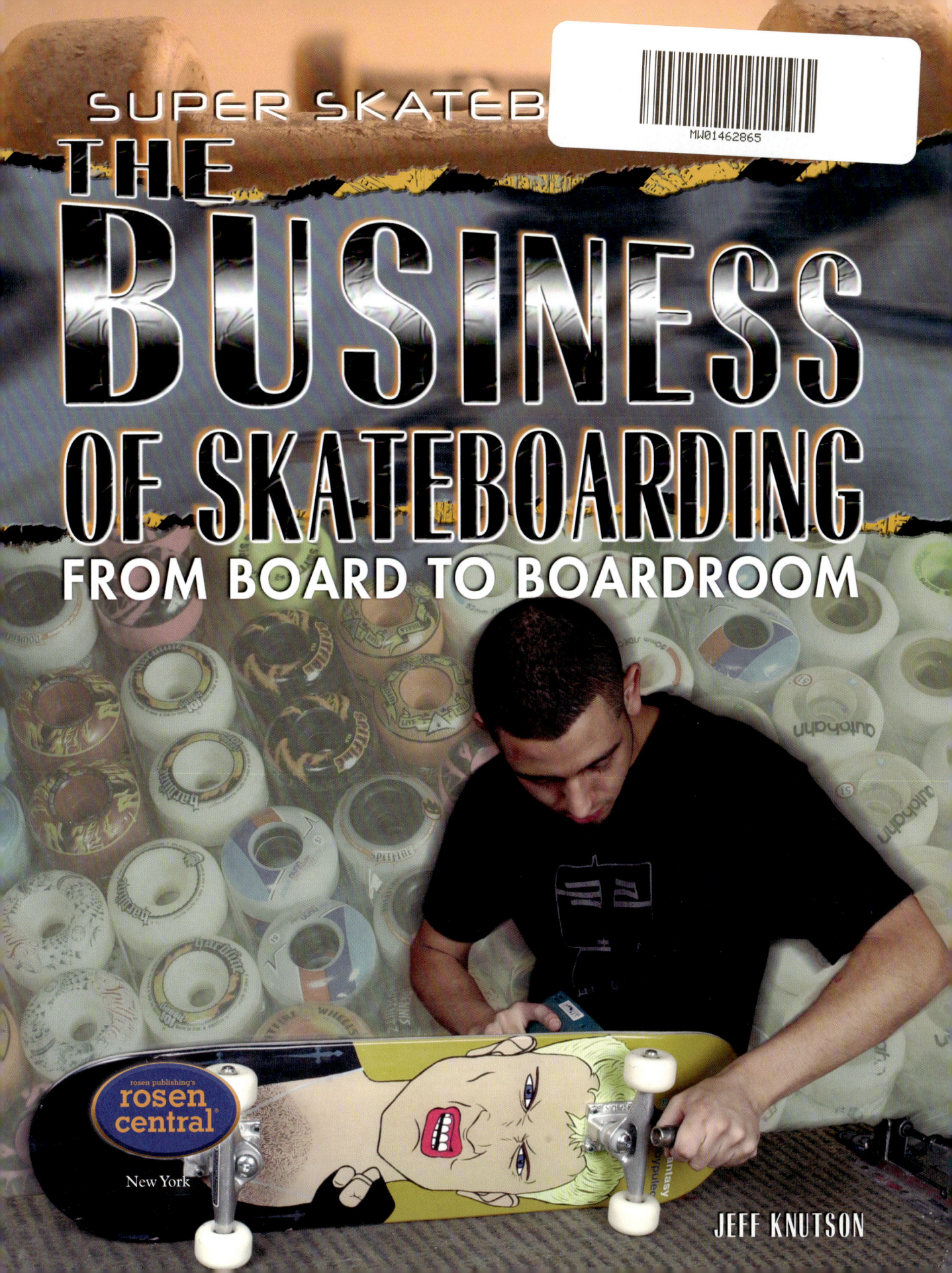

SUPER SKATEBOARDING

THE BUSINESS OF SKATEBOARDING
FROM BOARD TO BOARDROOM

rosen publishing's
rosen central
New York

JEFF KNUTSON

Published in 2009 by The Rosen Publishing Group, Inc.
29 East 21st Street, New York, NY 10010

Copyright © 2009 by The Rosen Publishing Group, Inc.

First Edition

All rights reserved. No part of this book may be reproduced in any form without permission in writing from the publisher, except by a reviewer.

Library of Congress Cataloging-in-Publication Data

Knutson, Jeff.
 The business of skateboarding: from board to boardroom / Jeff Knutson.—1st ed.
   p. cm.—(Super skateboarding)
 Includes bibliographical references.
 ISBN-13: 978-1-4358-5051-4 (library binding)
 ISBN-13: 978-1-4358-5395-9 (pbk)
 ISBN-13: 978-1-4358-5401-7 (6 pack)
 1. Skateboarding—Juvenile literature. 2. Skateboarding—Economic aspects—Juvenile literature. 3. Skateboards—Design and construction—Juvenile literature. I. Title.
 GV859.8.K65 2009
 796.22—dc22

2008017842

Manufactured in the United States of America

On the cover: A skateboard shop employee attaches the trucks to a newly assembled skateboard.

Contents

Introduction 4

Chapter One: Getting the Goods Out 9

Chapter Two: Skate Media 17

Chapter Three: The Profession of Skateboarding 25

Chapter Four: Skate Shops and Skate Parks 33

Glossary 41

For More Information 42

For Further Reading 44

Bibliography 45

Index 46

INTRODUCTION

Working in a skate shop is fun. It's part of the industry that skaters know the best. But there are many other jobs in the skateboarding industry as well.

If you are interested in skateboarding, then you have found a sport that is both fun and exciting. Skateboarding attracts many athletic and creative individuals who are extremely talented, and these people have pushed skateboarding to become the totally amazing sport it is today. Many people even consider skateboarding to be more of an art than a sport. And for some, skateboarding can become a whole lifestyle. But for a growing number of skilled and dedicated skaters, it can turn into something even more. With commitment and hard work, skateboarding can turn from a hobby into a career.

The skateboarding industry has grown a lot. As the industry grows, a lot of people are needed to do all of the jobs necessary to get boards under the feet of skaters. In fact, the skateboarding industry has grown so much that there are hundreds—maybe even thousands—of different careers related to skateboarding that someone could do for his or her work. Today, there are skateboarders everywhere who go to work day-in and day-out just like everyone else. The only difference is that these people get to do one of the totally radical jobs within the skateboarding industry. Of course, it isn't all fun and games, or 5-0 grinds and kick-flips. People in the skateboarding industry work as hard as they skate—and skating is what keeps it all going.

In the beginning, the skateboarding world was small. There were only a handful of true skateboarders who mostly lived on the West Coast, in Southern California. Skateboarding was born out of surfing, and many of the first skateboard companies were actually surfboard companies that made skateboards on the side. These companies catered to surfers who needed something to do when the waves were bad. Most of these companies were very small, and they were usually owned and operated by a single

Everything a skater needs is supplied by the skateboarding industry, from boards, trucks, and wheels to pads, clothing, and accessories.

skateboarder or surfer. This owner might have hired a friend or two to help out around the shop, probably one of his or her surfing or skating buddies. Not only was skateboarding simply a hobby, but the building and selling of skateboards were more of a hobby as well.

Over time, however, as the popularity of skateboarding began to take off, more and more people wanted to skate and buy skateboards. Demand for skateboards and related equipment increased. Surf shops began to carry and sell more skateboarding gear, from boards, trucks and wheels to kneepads, helmets and even clothes.

At the same time, surf companies started focusing more on skateboarding. Thanks in large part to the legendary Z-Boys of Malibu, California, who were featured in the award-winning 2001 documentary movie *Dogtown and Z-Boys*, the popularity of skateboarding skyrocketed in the 1970s and early 1980s. Soon, skateboard-specific shops started popping up all over California and the rest of the country. All the while, new companies dedicated to skateboarding started making skateboards and gear, producing skate-related products, and catering to the specific needs of skateboarders everywhere.

The legendary Tony Alva performs one of the first ever frontside airs in 1977. Alva rode for the Zephyr Skateboard team and later started his own company, called Alva Skateboards.

Today, the skateboarding industry is huge. The next time you are in a skateboard shop, take a look at the boards that are displayed on the wall. Have you ever wondered what makes each of them unique? Naturally, some boards just look cooler than others because of the graphics, or designs, on the boards. And some of them are slightly different in shape compared to the others. Very few companies actually build skateboard decks in the United States today. Most skating equipment and clothing that we buy today are manufactured overseas or in Mexico. But the designs and the concepts of these products all come from companies here in the United States; these companies are known as distributors.

Because the skateboarding industry is so huge, there are a lot of different skateboard-related jobs that a person could do. This book will highlight the hottest and newest jobs in the field and the totally unique people who have made careers for themselves in the world of skateboarding.

CHAPTER ONE
GETTING THE GOODS OUT

When you are skateboarding, it's easy to take your board for granted. Whether you are grinding an awesome ledge with your friends, sessioning a mini-ramp, or ripping through the bowl at the skate park, you're probably just focused on staying on your board. Sometimes, it can be easy to forget what makes your particular board setup unique to the way that you skate.

Skateboard distribution companies do the work of designing a multitude of products and then getting the boards, trucks, wheels, and other goods from the factories and into the hands—and under the feet—of skaters everywhere. Most skateboard distributors deal not only with skateboard decks but also with trucks, wheels, bearings, and other skate equipment—what people in the industry call "hardgoods." Additionally, most distributors handle what are called "softgoods" as well—things like T-shirts, hats, clothing, and even other products such as stickers and posters.

Needless to say, skateboard distribution companies do a lot of work. Skateboard distributors are at the hub of the skateboard industry wheel. Much more than a middleman, a skateboard distribution company connects the skaters with the boards, and there are a lot of cool jobs to be done there.

But a distribution company doesn't just design and organize the goods. Every skate shop purchases almost all of the skateboards it sells

Distribution companies do a lot of work. They design, market, ship, and sometimes even manufacture all of the parts and accessories sold in skate shops.

from a number of major skateboard distributors. In fact, a lot of the time, a distribution company will work specifically with a few skateboard brands, distributing only their boards. On another front, distributors also create advertising for specific skate brands.

A great example of a distributor that works with specific brands is Deluxe Distribution, in San Francisco, California. Deluxe produces skateboards and trucks for different companies, such as Real Skateboards, Anti-Hero Skateboards, Thunder Trucks, and Spitfire Wheels.

Most distribution companies operate out of a warehouse with some offices attached, and there are usually a lot of different people doing all sorts of jobs there—much like any other type of warehouse. From the office workers in the sales, advertising and accounting departments to the warehouse workers doing shipping and receiving duties, there is a lot to be done.

But the coolest and most sought-after jobs at a skateboard distribution company are almost always the ones that involve the skateboard teams. The skateboard teams aren't just the pro skaters themselves. They also include team photographers, videographers, and team managers. Of course, these jobs are so cool because they are the ones that actually involve the act of skateboarding. Oftentimes, these people also work closely with a company's marketing and advertising departments, helping to develop new products, forecasting and creating what will become the newest trends in the skateboarding world.

Let's take a look at some of the different aspects of these fun and interesting jobs.

Graphics and Design

Even the most hard-core skater will tell you that a big part of the skateboarding world has to do with how you and your board look.

The Business of Skateboarding: From Board to Boardroom

Skateboarding is all about image—it's not just what you do, but how you do it that makes a difference. As artistic athletes, skateboarders are unique. They want to have boards, equipment, and clothes that reflect their own individualized sense of who they are. If they wanted to wear a uniform and look like everybody else, then they would just play a team sport such as football or soccer. But skaters are different; skaters want to stand out from the crowd. A lot of skaters may even select a board simply because they like the graphic—or artistic design—painted on the bottom of the deck. They may pick out a T-shirt because it has a unique logo that will make them look cool.

Skateboard graphics have always been an important part of the sport and part of what gives skateboarding its counterculture image.

Getting the Goods Out

How these graphics are created and then painted on the bottoms of skateboard decks, screen-printed on T-shirts, and embroidered on hats and other gear is an interesting story. Occasionally, the skaters themselves are often hired to design the graphics for their own pro-model boards. Since skaters are usually creative people, it makes sense that a pro skater who has great skills on a board might also have some talent with a paintbrush or pen. However, pro skaters don't design most of the skateboard graphics and logos that are out there. Generally, professional graphic designers who also happen to be skateboarders create these graphics and logos.

Graphic designers work in almost every industry, but they are especially essential to skateboarding because that particular industry is so image-driven. A graphic

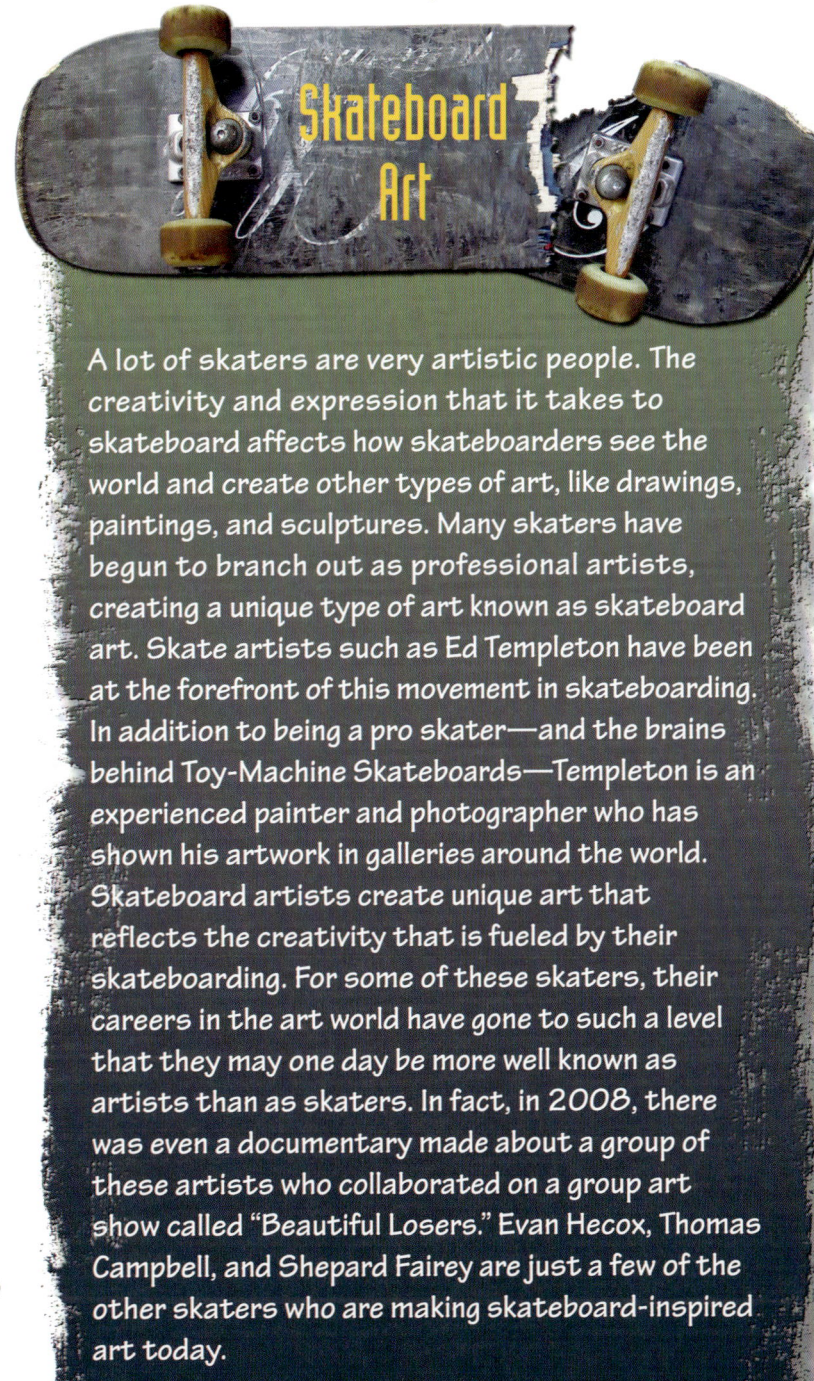

Skateboard Art

A lot of skaters are very artistic people. The creativity and expression that it takes to skateboard affects how skateboarders see the world and create other types of art, like drawings, paintings, and sculptures. Many skaters have begun to branch out as professional artists, creating a unique type of art known as skateboard art. Skate artists such as Ed Templeton have been at the forefront of this movement in skateboarding. In addition to being a pro skater—and the brains behind Toy-Machine Skateboards—Templeton is an experienced painter and photographer who has shown his artwork in galleries around the world. Skateboard artists create unique art that reflects the creativity that is fueled by their skateboarding. For some of these skaters, their careers in the art world have gone to such a level that they may one day be more well known as artists than as skaters. In fact, in 2008, there was even a documentary made about a group of these artists who collaborated on a group art show called "Beautiful Losers." Evan Hecox, Thomas Campbell, and Shepard Fairey are just a few of the other skaters who are making skateboard-inspired art today.

designer is like an artist, but instead of simply painting or drawing for the sake of art, he or she creates and designs artwork that can be used on products and in advertising. Skateboard companies hire graphic designers who create graphics and logos that end up on boards, wheels, clothing, and other gear. And not only that, but a graphic designer hired to work for a skateboard company might also help create the layout of a full-page ad that could end up in next month's issue of *Transworld* magazine.

However, some skateboard artists and graphic designers are people who aren't pro skaters necessarily, but they are professional graphic designers that happen to skate. Some skateboard companies have a full-time graphic designer (or maybe even a few of them) on staff. A good example of this is seen with Girl and Chocolate skateboards, which have a collection of designers that call themselves the Art Dump. Some companies may hire different freelance graphic designers for different jobs.

The Freedom of Freelancing

People who "work freelance" don't work for any one company. Rather, they work for themselves, running their own graphic design companies. Many graphic designers in the skateboarding industry only work as freelancers so that they can also do work for other, non-skateboard-related companies on the side. Many skateboard companies and magazines may hire a different designer for each design job, depending on what kind of style they are looking for. Even though most graphic designers are freelancers, almost all of them that work in the skateboarding industry have a personal connection to skateboarding. While some of these graphic designers used to work exclusively for a skate company, others might be avid skaters who have friends and connections in the industry, which helps them land different design jobs.

Shoe design and sales are an important part of the skateboarding industry. Skate shoe companies continually design and produce new shoe styles in order to stay on the cutting edge of the sport.

Tech Tricks for Designers

Today, graphic design is a very digitally oriented job. Even when photographs, paintings, or other types of artistic drawings are used, these graphics will always be scanned into a digital file and edited on a computer. Much like skate photographers, graphic designers need to be experienced with state-of-the-art computer programs such as Photoshop and Illustrator, both of which are made by Adobe. These computer programs are highly complicated and take a lot of time to learn. For this reason, graphic design is a job that takes a lot of complex computer skills, as well as patience and attention to detail. Fortunately, skateboarders are detail-oriented people by nature. Any skater can tell you that failure to pay attention to the smallest details, like tiny pebbles or cracks in the concrete, can be disastrous! This might be why so many skaters end up working in such detail-oriented fields.

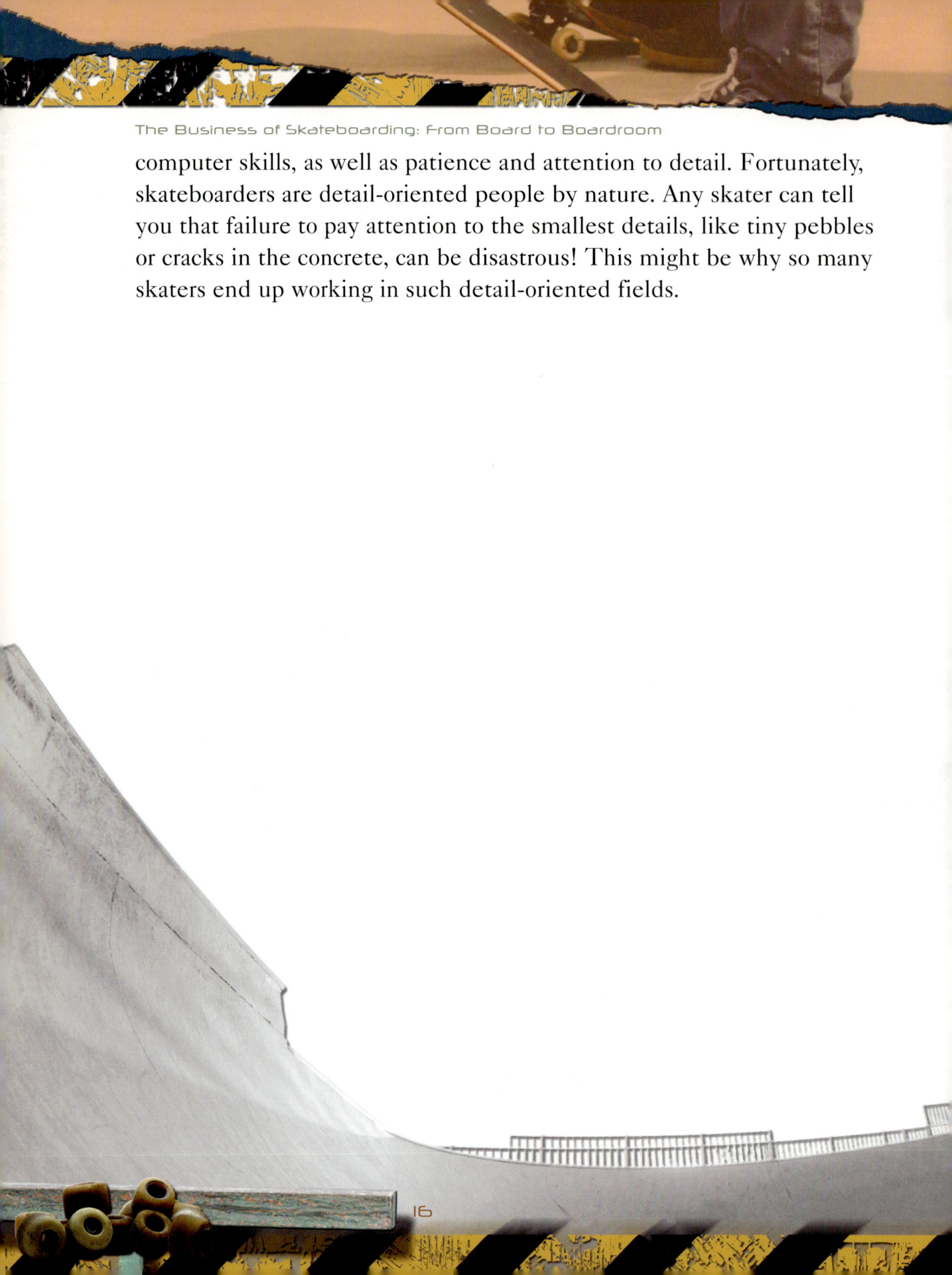

CHAPTER TWO
SKATE MEDIA

It's almost as amazing to watch skateboarding as it is to actually skate. Even people who have never skateboarded love to watch it. And most skaters can admit to having spent countless hours flipping through magazine pages, checking out what other skaters are doing. From pictures of pros accomplishing incredible feats to sequences of the most amazing lines, or series of tricks, to shots of the coolest spots, photos have propelled the sport of skateboarding. Today, the job of a skateboard photographer is to produce dynamic photos of the pros doing what they do best. But as the skateboarding world has grown, so has the job of skateboard photographer.

First and foremost, professional skateboard photographers simply need to be exceptional photographers. They not only need to be very experienced in using cameras, lenses, and lighting equipment, but they also need to be able to understand skateboarding in a way that only a skateboarder can. Most of all, skateboard photographers need to have the innate ability to document skateboarding in a way that portrays it as the raw and extreme sport that it is.

How It All Started

Early photographers such as Glen E. Friedman (who took many famous photos of Southern California's Z-Boys team in the 1970s) and *Thrasher* magazine's "MoFo" set the stage for skateboard photography today. These photographers were able to take amazing pictures of the best skaters simply because they knew the skaters. In fact, the photographers themselves were skaters. This fact is still an important part of being a skateboard photographer today. When pro skaters are out at a spot on a photo shoot, there is often a lot of pressure on them to land tricks and push themselves harder than ever before. In order to capture these shots, it is important that a skateboard photographer understands what is going through a skater's mind.

Skate Photography Today and Into the Future

Skate photographers have to think about a lot of other things as well. They have to deal with a lot of the same issues in their work that many other outdoor sports photographers deal with, like lighting, picking the right lens and camera angle, dealing with changing weather, and, of course, getting the most amazing shots while staying out of the skater's way. For instance, a skater might be attempting a difficult bank-to-wall ride in a narrow downtown alley. Unless the photographer can set up fast enough with the proper angle, the correct lighting, and the right camera settings before the skater even attempts the trick, there will be no photo.

When skating and photographing in the street, timing is everything. The session might be over before any shots are taken if the skaters find out that they aren't allowed to be there. Of course, the success of any skateboard photographer also hinges on the performance of their subjects—the skaters.

Suppose a day of skating and photographing goes well. But when the skaters are done skating, the photographer's job is far from over. Almost all skate photography today is done digitally, and the photo files need to be uploaded into a computer and then edited before they can

In the fast-paced world of skateboarding, every millisecond counts. Timing is everything for skateboard photographers who want to capture images with the most action.

be sent to a magazine or used in an advertisement. Skate photographers will often spend hours searching through their photo files, looking for just the right shot to use.

Once they have found the perfect picture, the editing work begins. Most professional photographers, including skateboard photographers, use professional photo-editing computer programs such as Adobe Photoshop. These computer programs allow the photographer to crop photos (or cut off the edges to enlarge them) and use other special effects, such as color correction to brighten up and highlight the most exciting parts of the photograph.

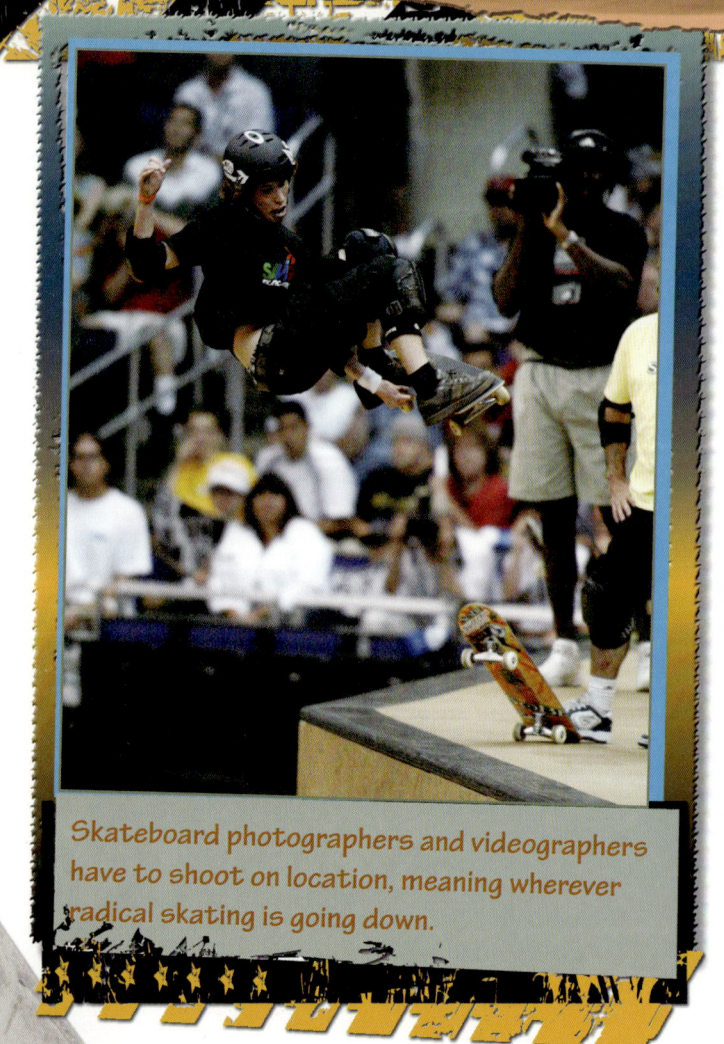

From acting quickly on the spot behind the camera to patiently editing and selecting photos behind a computer monitor, being a skateboard photographer requires many different skills and talents. In the end, though, it is fun and rewarding work.

Skate Videographer

While it is amazing to look at photos of skateboarding, videos of skateboarding can be even more attention grabbing. Most skateboard videos today are produced by individual skate teams as a way to help promote their products. However, many other videos might be produced by skate magazines, individual skate shops, or even groups of amateur skaters that decide to make their own video.

Classic skate videos, such as the Bones Brigade's *The Search for Animal Chin* and Blind's popular *Video Days*, set the stage for many of the skate videos to follow. More than just good skate footage set to music, these videos contain humor, drama, suspense, and even a storyline, making them all the more fun and exciting for skaters and others to watch.

Today's skate videos are produced using the most up-to-date technology, and, as a result, they look better than ever before. Skateboard videographers need a lot of the same skills that skateboard photographers

Skateboard photographers and videographers have to shoot on location, meaning wherever radical skating is going down.

need—not just to shoot the intense video footage but also to edit and produce the slick-looking videos that skaters will want to watch again and again. Skateboard videographers need visual and artistic sensibilities, and they need the technical skills to operate high-tech cameras and video-editing software. And, on top of everything, many videographers must shoot their footage while riding on top of a skateboard themselves!

Patience . . . to the Extreme!

As with a skateboard photographer, a videographer's job is far from done after the footage is shot. All of the raw and radical footage of the skaters attempting tricks has to be cut, edited, and set to a soundtrack. All of these editing tasks can be very fun and entertaining, but the work itself can be quite tedious as well. Being a videographer requires an extreme amount of patience and attention to detail. Also, most skate videographers today use top-of-the-line video editing software such as Apple's Final Cut Pro and a special program called Motion that allows them to use the amazing special effects that will make the skate video stand out from all the others.

The job of a skateboard videographer is both diverse and dynamic. From filming a pro doing a radical line while skating on your own board to spending hours in front of a computer monitor, skateboard videographers need many talents. Not only do they need extremely good skateboarding and camera-operating skills, but they must also have an eye for what looks good, as well as an ear for the hottest new music to use as a soundtrack for all of the radical skateboarding footage.

Skateboarding Magazines

Since the beginning of skateboarding, magazines on the topic have been a valuable resource for skaters everywhere. From Craig Stecyk's famous

The Business of Skateboarding: From Board to Boardroom

Spike Jonze

From skateboarding to Hollywood: In 1991, Blind Skateboards, the seminal skateboard company then operated by pro skater Mark Gonzalez, released a video that became a piece of skateboarding history. The video, called *Video Days*, features the early skateboarding of Gonzalez, as well as other famed skaters such as Jason Lee and Guy Mariano. A young friend of the Gonz named Spike Jonze directed the video. Jonze himself was a skater. He was also a photographer/videographer for *Transworld Skateboarding* at the time. Jonze later went on to create music videos for bands including the Beastie Boys and Weezer, and he has even directed movies in Hollywood, some of which have been nominated for an Academy Award!

articles on the Z-Boys in *Skateboarder* magazine in the 1970s to the latest pro spotlights in the *Skateboard Mag* today, skateboarding magazines have played a large part in documenting the history—and propelling the future—of the sport. Not only that, but these magazines have also been a central part of what holds the skateboarding community together.

More than just news and reports, these magazines have played a big part in creating skate culture. Since its inception in the early 1980s, *Thrasher* magazine has been a beacon for skaters everywhere who are searching for the inside scoop on their unique subculture. *Thrasher* looks deep into skate culture, sometimes even containing artwork and short stories from famous skate creators such as Mark Gonzalez. But *Thrasher* certainly hasn't been the only skateboarding magazine that keeps skaters informed. Today, magazines such as *Transworld Skateboarding*, *Slap*, *Skateboarder*, and the *Skateboard Mag* are all frontrunners in the world of skateboard publications.

As many young skaters often turn the pages of skate magazines, poring over full-page photos of amazing spots and reading profiles and

Skateboard magazines help fuel interest in the sport. From photos to articles to editorials to advertising, a lot of work goes into each issue.

interviews with the raddest pros, they may be wondering just how a major skateboard magazine comes together. In fact, most of these magazines operate with a relatively small staff. Much like the skateboard distribution companies that were mentioned earlier, most skateboard magazines have their own photographers, videographers, and graphic designers. They may also hire freelancers to do this work. But the most important job at a skateboard magazine is that of an editor.

Editors Put It All Together

There may be a handful of different editors working on a magazine's staff. It is their job to determine what stories, interviews, photos, and advertisements make it into the magazine and how the finished product will look. Almost all magazine editors work full-time for their magazines and are not freelancers. Most of the articles, interviews, and other writing in a skateboard magazine is done by the editors, although this work will occasionally be contracted out to a freelance writer or, sometimes, to a pro skateboarder who has a story to tell.

In the Know

Aside from great writing skills, editors need to have a strong sense of what is happening in the skateboarding world. Skateboard magazine editors usually have inside contacts within the skateboard companies—often with people such as team managers—who will keep them informed of what the companies and the pros are up to. This is helpful because an editor needs to have his or her finger on the pulse of the skateboarding world. Editors make sure that each month's issue is up to date, not just with the latest news but also with a style that represents the current trends in the skateboarding world.

More than anything, the editor of a skateboard magazine needs the same skills that any magazine editor needs: a sense of how information should be presented to a wide range of readers, a strong grasp of the English language, and a knack for telling a good story.

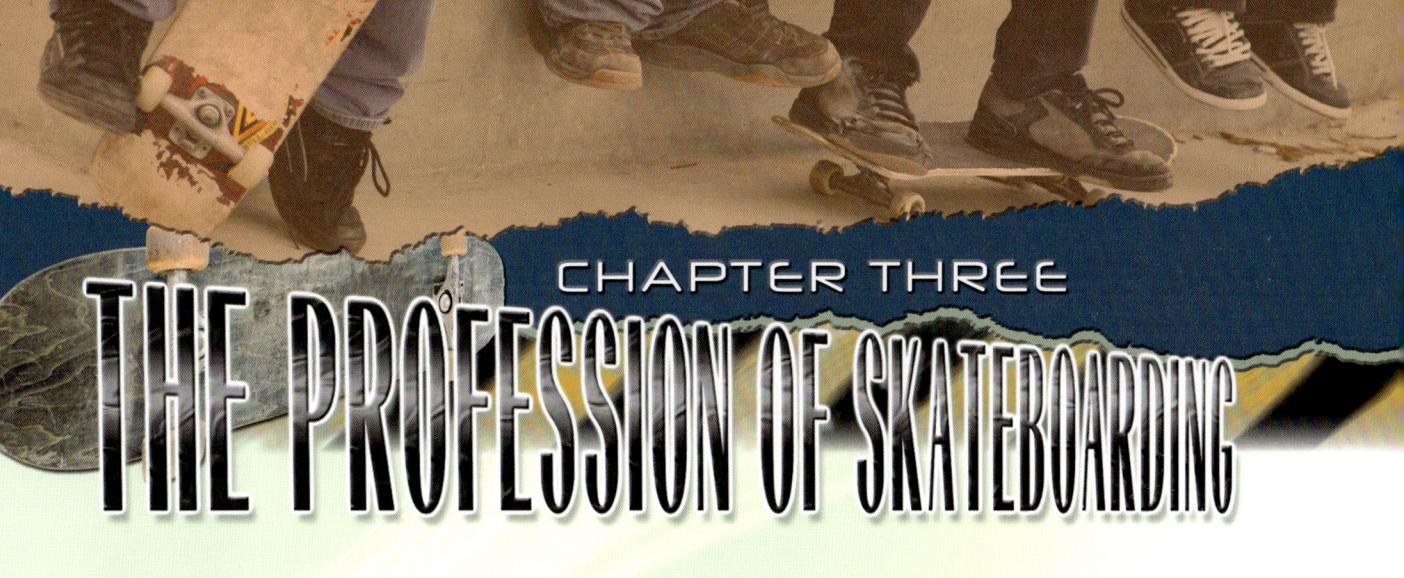

CHAPTER THREE
THE PROFESSION OF SKATEBOARDING

"Professional skateboarder" is a job title that only a very few, extremely talented individuals get to have. To become a professional skateboarder takes an insane mix of talents: an extreme amount of physical skill, hard-core mental drive, obsessive stick-to-itiveness, and perhaps some luck thrown in for good measure. There are a lot of very talented skateboarders out there in the world, and not all of them get to become professionals in the sport.

Being a professional skateboarder is not only a means to make money and a name for yourself, but it is also a way to help skateboard companies and other sponsors promote their products. While some pro skaters still make money through winning skate contests, most pros today make most of their money through product endorsements and sponsorships. For this reason, most skate companies want to hire professionals who are not only the most amazing skaters but are also individuals who personify an image that represents the company.

Skate Like a Pro, Look Like a Pro

As an example, a skater such as Tony Trujillo—who is best known for his radical punk-rock style and speedy, high-flying airs—may win a few contests each year, sometimes earning a significant amount of money.

Tony Trujillo's name is synonymous with that of his sponsors and magazines such as *Thrasher*, which feature his skating.

But Trujillo is also sponsored by Anti-Hero Skateboards and the shoe company Vans. The Vans company even produces and sells pairs of special, pro-model shoes emblazoned with Trujillo's name. The term "pro-model" means that a professional skater has endorsed that particular product and uses it to skate. Whether a skateboard deck, a pair of shoes, or any other product that a skate company might sell—even T-shirts and jackets—pro skaters make the majority of their income by endorsing products. Every time a pro skater appears in an advertisement, skating with his or her pro-model board, wearing his or her pro-model shoes, or sporting the company's latest T-shirt, that skater gets paid by the company. Also, in some cases, pro skaters get paid what is known as a royalty. For instance, when a skateboarder gets paid a royalty for a pro-model board that he or she endorses, it means that the skater gets paid a small amount for each board that is sold in stores.

Skateboarding Business Trips

Skate companies want to sell as many boards and other products as possible, and they often schedule lots of photo and video shoots for

Part of Shaun White's job is to promote his sponsors' products. From stickers on boards and helmets to T-shirt designs with brand names, the pros are helping to spread a company's identity.

their pros to keep them busy. Oftentimes, these companies even choose to send their professional skaters together as a team to exotic locations around the world just to skate and get photos and video footage. Because of this, being a pro skater can involve quite a bit of traveling. Getting paid to travel the world to skate is definitely one of the coolest parts of being a professional skater. However, it is important to keep in mind that pro skaters are under a lot of pressure to perform. Imagine if a skate company paid for you to fly all the way to Barcelona, Spain, for a weeklong filming trip, but then you had a bad week and didn't land many tricks. Because of these types of difficulties, the pros that do the best are the ones who are both versatile and consistent in their skating.

While being a professional skater can be one of the most demanding and high-pressure jobs in the industry, it can come with the rewards of fame, the excitement of travel, and the once-in-a-lifetime experience of getting paid to do what you love.

Team Manager

One of the most amazing things about watching a skate video is that so much of the skating seems spontaneous and natural. It's almost as if the skater, the photographer, and the videographer were all in the right place at exactly the right time, and then skated away with some awesome footage. Sometimes, this is exactly what happens because skateboarding is such a creative and off-the-wall activity. But more often than not, there is a great deal of planning that goes into the filming of a skate video. And not only that, but there is even more planning that goes into the day-to-day lives of pro skaters on a skate team. A team manager does most of this planning. The team manager also does other kinds of jobs, like scheduling photo shoots or organizing skate demos and other events for the company. Most of all, the team manager is the one who

Professional skate teams work together to push each other's skating and pull off amazing moves. Every skate team has a team manager who helps to organize skate sessions and photo shoots.

keeps everyone on the skate team on schedule. Simply put, the team manager is the glue that holds a skate team together.

Smooth Operator

Being a team manager is a fun and challenging job that requires a whole host of different skills. For instance, on any given day a team manager might organize a skate session with all of the pros from the team at a local spot. He or she might also invite a magazine photographer to cover the session. This would mean that the team manager has to arrange for all of the skaters and the photographer to show up at the same place at the same time, which is often more difficult than it sounds. A lot of the time, this means that the team manager might have to drive around, pick up each skater at his or her house, and then bring them all to the spot, hopefully in time to meet the photographer. Once the team is at the spot, ollieing and grinding away, if the skate spot happens to be on private property, the team manager is the one who potentially will have to deal with angry property owners and maybe even the police. Needless to say, a team manager needs to be a "people person." One of the most important skills that he or she can possess is the ability to be diplomatic.

Travel Agent

On a day-to-day level, the job of a team manager can vary quite a bit because skate teams and pro skaters are always up to something different. Whether setting up a day of filming at a local spot, planning a demo in another state, organizing an overseas filming trip, or driving the team van on a cross-country road trip, the team manager is a busy person. The number one duty of a team manager is coordination. In addition to being able to get along with many different types of people, it is also important for team managers to work well on the phone and through e-mail when coordinating all the different activities.

Team managers do lots of extra work as well. For instance, during downtime, when the skaters and photo crew are working, a team manager's job can vary from helping to shoot backup photos and video, to picking up water and snacks for the skaters. Most team managers are usually fairly experienced, if not expert, skaters themselves. They need to know every detail of how to find a great skate spot and what makes a skate session fun.

A career in skateboarding can take you to strange places. Rob Dyrdek (*left*) and his pal, Chris Boykin, even had their own reality show on MTV.

Another challenging facet of the team manager's job is that he or she is responsible for keeping the skaters happy, safe, and healthy. This can mean finding the team riders a place to live in a cool neighborhood, or setting them up with the hottest new clothes to wear. But it can also take the form of managing and handing out the pros' per diem—or daily—money while on tours, keeping the team riders out of trouble, and being a responsible van driver.

Being a team manager takes a lot of personality, creativity, dependability, and responsibility. The multiple roles involved in doing a team manager's job can be a handful. Getting a radical pro skater and a great skate photographer to show up at a sick skate spot at the same time can be difficult, and the manager's efforts in doing so are often underappreciated. But when all the pieces fall into place, and photos of pro skaters end up on the covers of major skateboard magazines, great team managers are able to shine and take pride in the fact that they are the ones who made it all come together.

CHAPTER FOUR
SKATE SHOPS AND SKATE PARKS

The skate shop is where everything in the skateboarding industry comes together for the skater. Brand-new decks with glimmering graphics hang on the wall. Colorful wheels and trucks are lined up in perfect rows in the display case. All of the newest shoes are carefully arranged, just waiting to be skated. The displays, clothing racks, and walls are filled with examples of the latest technology and the hottest new products. The collective work of every person in the skateboarding industry is showcased at the skate shop.

As a skateboarder, perhaps you have wondered what it would be like to work in the wonderland that is a skate shop. Working in a skate shop is probably the most accessible job in the industry for young skaters. For them, the skate shop may represent much more than any other type of shop.

More Than Just a Shop

On the surface, a skate shop is simply a retail store just like any other. Working there requires many of the same skills that anyone would need for other types of retail-oriented jobs: strong customer service skills, experience using a cash register, and a knack for keeping the place organized so that the products are properly displayed. However, since a skate shop is different, there are some extra duties for the employees

Skaters can be picky when it comes to purchasing boards and other equipment. Skate shops usually carry a wide variety of products to please every skater.

who work at one. Most skate shop employees should know how to put boards together for customers, make recommendations about accessories that customers might want, and help grip-tape a board before it goes out the door. All of this takes experience with skating, and most skate shop employees are experienced skaters.

But as any skater can tell you, the skate shop is more than just a store; it serves as a community center for all of the local skaters. This aspect creates extra responsibilities for the employees. Oftentimes, skaters will use a skate shop as a meeting place where they can get

In addition to hanging out with the locals and recommending products to customers, skate shop employees are also responsible for setting up and assembling new boards.

ready for a day of skating or reflect upon the session that just went down. Other times, skaters might simply come to the skate shop to hang out, socialize, and be a part of the local scene. On any given day, skate shop employees might find themselves playing video games, watching new skate videos, or even playing a game of *Skate* on the front sidewalk with some locals. In this way, working at a skate shop is not only different, but it is also a lot of fun as well.

While working in a skate shop is definitely fun, it can also be a great way to learn about all the facets of the skateboarding world. Skate shop employees can keep up to date on all of the latest trends and products, giving them a good foundation of knowledge about the industry. Working at such a shop might even be a great place to start a career in the skateboarding world.

How Skate Parks Are Created

To some, it may seem like designing a skate park would be as simple as making an abstract painting—a guessing game of concrete peaks and valleys that anyone could make. However, nothing could be further from the truth. For today's top skate park designers, creating a skate park is an exacting science, requiring years of experience, top-notch landscape design skills, and exact knowledge of what skaters want. Two of the world's best skate park design-and-construction companies are Dreamland Skateparks of Lincoln City, Oregon, and Grindline skate parks based out of Seattle, Washington. Both of these companies are entirely owned and operated by expert skateboarders who understand precisely how a great skate park should look. These workers pay attention to each and every detail of how their skate parks are designed, built, and skated.

Concrete parks, such as Lincoln City Skatepark, are growing in popularity because of their innovative designs.

While most skate park designers get to spend a considerable amount of time skating, they do most of their design work indoors, with an intimate knowledge of the latest computer-aided design software and experience in the field of landscape architecture. Most skate park designers have been skate park builders at one time or another, and they also have experience with the construction portion of the job. In fact, many skate park designers still help in the actual construction of the parks. It is crucial for skate park designers to know if the contours, banks, hips, bowls, and cradles that they design on computer screens and paper blueprints will actually be possible to build in the real world.

Humble Beginnings

Many of the world's top skate park builders got their start by building backyard ramps when they were younger. Some of them even started by pouring their own concrete obstacles. For example, the skate park designers Mark "Red" Scott and Sage Bolyard, who both design parks for Dreamland, were some of the original builders and skaters at the legendary Burnside Skatepark underneath the Burnside Bridge in Portland, Oregon. Back in the early 1990s, Scott and Bolyard, along with a handful of other very dedicated skaters, needed a place to skate during the rainy Portland winters. Without the city's permission, they began to sculpt concrete into transitions that could be skated. These transitions went up against the pillars underneath the bridge. Little by little, the skaters from Burnside not only constructed an entire skate park under the bridge, but they managed to create a place known worldwide as one of the premiere places to skate. With its newfound notoriety, and with some help from community members and a progressive mayor named Bud Clark, the area was ultimately recognized by the city as an official skate park, kind of like a community garden made of concrete.

Skate Shops and Skate Parks

Building Dreams

Today, the builders of parks such as the ones constructed by Dreamland and Grindline are hard workers and dedicated skaters to the core. Just like learning to skate, building a skate park is a very labor-intensive activity that takes a lot of practice in order to perfect. Skate park builders move tons of dirt and sculpt concrete into the smooth curves, perfect transitions, precision ledges, and other obstacles. This work involves a lot of physical labor, strength, heavy lifting, and experience in the construction field. Most of the people who work in skate park

This park built by Grindline in Trinidad, Colorado, includes features like an over-vert bowl, great coping, perfect concrete, and endless lines for skaters of all ages.

construction are excellent skaters themselves. The urge to skate an unfinished park is something that would undoubtedly drive many skaters mad. When most of us see a skate park, the very first thing we want to do is skate in it. But from beginning to end, the skate park construction process may take months. Because of this, working a skate park construction job takes a lot of patience as well. However, most skate park builders take pride in knowing that they have helped bring an awesome park to the communities in which they work. Skate park builders know that, even after they leave, moving on to the next project in a different town, they have set the stage for a whole new generation of skaters that will become hooked on the sport.

    Much like learning to skateboard, building a skate park is a process that takes a great deal of patience, imagination, a vision of the future, and a belief that anything is possible if you set your mind to it.

GLOSSARY

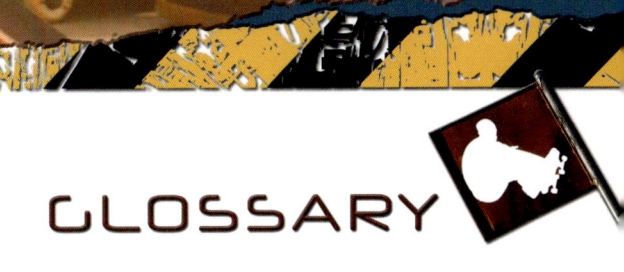

distributor A company involved in the design, production, marketing, and distribution of equipment and memorabilia.

freelancer A worker who is hired on a temporary basis by a company to do a particular job.

graphic designer A person who uses artistic and computer design skills to create graphics, logos, advertising, and other visuals for a company or magazine.

grip tape A sandpaper-like sheet with a strong adhesive on one side that can be applied to the top of a skateboard deck.

hardgoods The actual skateboarding equipment produced and sold by skateboard companies, like skateboard decks, trucks, and wheels.

session The act of skateboarding with one or more other skaters, sometimes organized by skateboard teams so that photographers can take pictures of the skaters.

skateboard art Artwork created by a skateboarder that is influenced by the skateboard culture.

softgoods The clothing, accessories, and other secondary products produced and sold by a skateboard company.

team manager A person hired by a skateboard company to manage a team of professional skaters.

videographer A person who films, edits, and produces videos, usually for a skateboard company or team, or for a skateboard magazine.

For More Information

The Art Dump
22500 S. Vermont
Torrance, CA 90502
Web site: http://www.theartdump.com

The Girl and Chocolate skateboard companies have an art department called the Art Dump. Not only do the employees design boards and other products, take amazing photographs, and produce some of the industry's best videos, but they run this cool Web site as well.

Deluxe Distribution
1111A 17th Street
San Francisco, CA 94107
(415) 468-7045
Web site: http://www.dlxsf.com

This is the Web site for all things Deluxe—from Anti-Hero and Real skateboard decks to Thunder Trucks and Spitfire Wheels. They've also got loads of information about upcoming events and what the different teams are up to.

Thrasher magazine
High Speed Productions
1303 Underwood Avenue
San Francisco, CA 94124
(415) 822-3083
Web site: http://www.thrashermagazine.com

Thrasher is all about hard-core skating. From interviews with the newest pros and photos of the gnarliest lines, to skate park information and reviews of the hottest new bands, *Thrasher* has it all.

Tobin Yelland
Photographer and Filmmaker
94 9th Street, 3rd Floor
Brooklyn, NY 11215
Web site: http://www.tobinyelland.com
Tobin Yelland's Web site offers a unique look into the world of a skater-turned-photographer-turned-filmmaker. With a vision as unique as anyone in the industry, Yelland continues to push the limits of creativity in the skateboarding world.

Transworld Skateboarding
Transworld Media
353 Airport Road
Oceanside, CA 92054
(760) 722-7777
Web site: http://www.skateboarding.com
An industry standard for more than a generation, *Transworld* is where skaters turn when they want to know what's happening in skateboarding. *Transworld* features interviews, photos, videos, and more.

Web Sites

Due to the changing nature of Internet links, Rosen Publishing has developed an online list of Web sites related to the subject of this book. This site is updated regularly. Please use this link to access the list:

http://www.rosenlinks.com/ssk/busk

FOR FURTHER READING

Barwin, Steven. *Sk8er*. Halifax, Canada: Lorimer, James & Company, Limited, 2008.

Brooke, Michael. *The Concrete Wave: The History of Skateboarding*. Toronto, Canada: Warwick Publishing, 1999.

Cliver, Sean. *Disposable: A History of Skateboard Art*. Corte Madera, CA: Ginko Press, 2007.

Hawk, Tony. *Hawk: Occupation: Skateboarder*. New York, NY: Regan Books, 2000.

Hocking, Justin. *Skate Parks*. New York, NY: Rosen Publishing, 2006.

Junor, Amy. *Skate!* New York, NY: DK Publishing, 2008.

McClellan, Ray. *Skateboard Vert*. New York, NY: Scholastic, 2008.

Rose, Aaron, et al. *Beautiful Losers: Contemporary Art and Street Culture*. New York, NY: D.A.P./Iconoclast, 2005.

Sievert, Terri. *Girls' Skateboarding*. Mankato, MN: Coughlan Publishing, 2007.

Streissguth, Thomas. *Skateboarding Street Style*. Eden Prairie, MN: Bellwether Media, 2008.

Thrasher magazine. *Thrasher: Insane Terrain*. New York, NY: Universe Publishing, 2001

Weyland, Jocko. *The Answer Is Never: A Skateboarder's History of the World*. New York, NY: Grove Press, 2002.

BIBLIOGRAPHY

Brooke, Michael. *The Concrete Wave: The History of Skateboarding.* Lynchburg, VA: Warwick House Publishing, 1999.

Hansen, Craig. Telephone Interview. March 3, 2008.

imdb.com. "Beautiful Losers." Retrieved March 7, 2008 (http://www.imdb.com/title/tt0430916/).

imdb.com. "Dogtown and Z-Boys." Retrieved March 8, 2008 (http://www.imdb.com/title/tt0275309/).

imdb.com. "Video Days." Retrieved March 8, 2008 (http://www.imdb.com/title/tt0375184/).

Reyes, Mickey. Personal Interview. March 3, 2008.

Shapiro, Jay. Personal Interview. March 2, 2008.

Weyland, Jocko. *The Answer Is Never: A Skateboarder's History of the World.* New York, NY: Grove Press, 2002.

INDEX

A
Art Dump, the, 14

B
Blind Skateboards, 22
Bolyard, Sage, 38
Burnside Skatepark, 38

C
Campbell, Thomas, 13

D
Deluxe Distribution, 11
Dogtown and Z-Boys, 6
Dreamland Skateparks, 36, 38, 39

E
editors, magazine, 23, 24
    skills needed, 24

F
Fairey, Shepard, 13
freelancers, 14, 23, 24
Friedman, Glen E., 17

G
Gonzalez, Mark, 22
graphic designers, 13–14, 23
    and digital age, 15–16
graphics and design, 11–16
Grindline, 36, 39

H
hardgoods, 9
Hecox, Evan, 13

J
Jonze, Spike, 22

L
Lee, Jason, 22

M
magazines, skateboarding, 14, 17–18, 21–24
    role in skate culture, 22
Mariano, Guy, 22
"MoFo," 18

P
photographers, 11, 15, 17–20, 22, 23, 28, 29–30, 32
    pioneers in field of skateboarding, 17–18
    skills needed, 17, 18–19, 20
professional skaters, 11, 18, 21, 24, 25–32
    as artists/designers, 13
    and sponsorships/endorsements, 25, 26
    and travel, 28
    what it takes to be, 25
"pro-model" products, 13, 26

Index

S

Scott, Mark "Red," 38
Search for Animal Chin, The, 20
skateboard art, 13
skateboard distribution companies, 8, 9–11, 23, 26
    jobs in, 11–14
Skateboarder magazine, 22
skateboarding industry
    early days of, 5–6
    growth of, 6–7
    and skater individuality, 12
Skateboard Mag, the, 22
skateboard teams, 11, 20, 28–29
skate parks, 9, 36–40
    building, 38, 39–40
    designing, 36–38
skate shops, 6, 7, 9–11, 33–36
    skills needed to work in, 33–35
Slap magazine, 22
softgoods, 9
Stecyk, Craig, 21–22

T

team managers, 11, 24, 28–32
    skills needed, 29–30, 32
Templeton, Ed, 13
Thrasher magazine, 17–18, 22
Toy-Machine Skateboards, 13
Transworld Skateboarding magazine, 14, 22
Trujillo, Tony, 25–26

V

Video Days, 20, 22
videographers, 11, 20–21, 22, 23, 28
    skills needed, 20–21

Z

Z-Boys, 6, 17, 22

The Business of Skateboarding: From Board to Boardroom

About the Author

Jeff Knutson is a skateboarder, writer, and high school teacher living in San Francisco, California. He was also an editor of *Life and Limb: Skateboarders Write from the Deep End*, a book that was published in 2004 by Soft Skull Press.

Photo Credits

Cover (left) © www.istockphoto.com/RickBL; cover (right), pp. 1, 10 (all photos), 34, 35 BLADES Board & Skate, New York, NY. Photos by Cindy Reiman; p. 3 © www.istockphoto.com/Shane White; pp. 4–5 © www.istockphoto.com/Richardson Maneze; pp. 4 (inset), 15, 27 © AP Images; p. 6 www.istockphoto.com/Kathleen and Scott Snowden; p. 7 Everett Collection; p. 12 Ray Tamarra/Getty Images; p. 19 Maura B. McConnell; p. 20 © Chris Polk/WireImages; p. 23 Marsaili McGrath/Getty Images for *Transworld*; p. 26 Adam Rountree/Getty Images; p. 29 J. Grant Brittain; p. 31 Frederick M. Brown/Getty Images; p. 37 courtesy *Thrasher* Magazine; p. 39 http://grindline.com; cover and interior background and decorative elements © www.istockphoto.com/ Dave Long, © www.istockphoto.com/David Kahn, © www.istockphoto.com/Alice Scully; © www.istockphoto.com/Leif Norman, © www.istockphoto.com/Ron Bailey; © www.istockphoto.com/jc559; © www.istockphoto.com/Reid Harrington; © www. istockphoto.com/Lora Clark.

Designer: Nelson Sá; Editor: Nicholas Croce
Photo Researcher: Cindy Reiman